SHUTTLE BUSES

Fleet History 1990–2020

David Granger

AMBERLEY

Front Cover (top): Ford Transit G188GSG passes under the railway arches in Kilmarnock in February 1993. (WMG)

Front Cover (bottom): MAN PO11HVX leaves Glasgow Science Centre on 07/16/18. (BN)

Rear Cover: Optare Solo YD63UZK passes Stagecoach Western Solo 47836 in Irvine on 29/04/19. (WMG)

First published 2020

Amberley Publishing
The Hill, Stroud
Gloucestershire, GL5 4EP

www.amberley-books.com

British Library Cataloguing in Publication Data.
A catalogue record for this book is available from the British Library.

ISBN 978 1 3981 0826 4 (print)
ISBN 978 1 3981 0827 1 (ebook)

Typesetting by SJmagic DESIGN SERVICES, India.
Printed in Great Britain.

Contents

Introduction

Prior to the deregulation of local bus services in 1986, Ayrshire was predominantly served by three long-established operators. The A1 Service co-operative could trace its roots back to the 1920s, and the similar AA Motor Services to the 1930s. The dominant operator, Western Scottish, which was still part of the state-owned Scottish Bus Group until 1991, was originally formed back in 1932.

During the years immediately following deregulation, the dominance of the establishment was challenged by a number of new-starts and existing coach companies moving into the local service market. Clyde Coast Coaches expanded their limited local service network into Kilmarnock; Keenans Coaches registered services in and around Ayr; Carrick Coaches was formed to operate inter-urban routes based in Ayr; and the Killie Hopper and Boyd's Handybus appeared on the scene to challenge Western in and around Kilmarnock. In 1990 two former employees of Western, David Granger and Harry Hay, formed Shuttle Buses, registering two routes based in Kilwinning and Troon.

With the takeovers of Western, A1 and AA by Stagecoach in the 1990s only one of these companies survives today – Shuttle Buses has outlived all its peers and over the past thirty years has developed into a successful and respected operator, still based in Kilwinning and still owned by one of its founders. The company now operates fifty-five vehicles throughout north, east and south Ayrshire on a variety of commercial and subsidised local services, along with Demand Responsive Transport operations in Ayrshire, Renfrewshire and Glasgow. A coaching arm trades as Shuttle Coaches.

Over 160 vehicles have passed through the fleet in that time. It started with two new Ford Transits, expanding with numerous second-hand Freight Rover Sherpas, and consolidated with Mercedes 709Ds. The local bus service fleet is now formed almost exclusively of Optare Solos. DRT services occupy more Solos (twenty-one are owned in total) along with a variety of lightweight models based on VW, Fiat and Mercedes chassis. A diverse coach fleet ranges from Ford Transits through Mercedes midicoaches, full-size Volvos, Scanias and KingLongs, to high-capacity MANs. The final Leyland Tiger was sold into preservation in 2019 and a Plaxton-bodied AEC Reliance dating from 1979 remains in occasional PSV service.

Shuttle Buses founders Harry Hay (left) and David Granger at the start of the journey in 1990. Sadly, Harry passed away in 1991, just as the company was becoming established.

During the past thirty years there has been one constant – Dormobile-bodied Ford Transit G831RDS, which operated the company's first ever journey on 2 January 1990, has remained in the fleet throughout. As part of the celebrations of achieving thirty years in business, this bus is being restored as an enduring tribute to Shuttle Buses' interesting and diverse fleet.

The 1990s

Ford Transits weren't our first choice, but three weeks before the start of services the company had no vehicles; George Steele of Blythswood Motors came to the rescue, providing two new Dormobile-bodied Transits for just £500 deposit on each. Fortunately, these proved to be very reliable vehicles, the only lost mileage in the first month of operations coming from a puncture, with maintenance being carried out by the Ford dealer in Kilmarnock in the evening. However, running two buses six days a week without a spare was never going to work in the long term and so a backup was purchased very quickly in the form of a Freight Rover Sherpa – the legendary but unloved 'breadvan' which played such an important role in the early days of deregulation in the shift from infrequent big bus services to frequent minibuses. Unpopular with drivers and passengers alike, this vehicle was cheap and surprisingly reliable, prompting the purchase of three more. Two were very rare Aitken-bodied examples from the defunct Inverness Traction. Reliability of these three was very disappointing and so another new Transit was added, bringing the fleet strength up to seven at the end of 1990.

Further expansion was limited by the poor financial performance of the business – a loss of £25,000 on a turnover of £139,000 was recorded for the first twelve months and 1991 was worse, revenue increasing to £236,000 but losses to £30,500. However, we decided that we had to grow in order to survive, and the fleet continued to grow rapidly. Two very unusual acquisitions were a pair of Talbot Pullman tri-axle minibuses, their short stay in the fleet reflecting their poor reliability. By 1992 the business was breaking even and a step change in vehicle quality came when two new Mercedes 29-seaters arrived. These were supplemented by more second-hand Sherpas and Transits. Boyd's provided a Bristol LHS and Bedford YMQ for a subsidised local service, both being the only examples of these chassis ever owned. An ambitious restoration project was former London Transport AEC Regal RF296, but sadly this was never completed.

School contracts saw the arrival of the first double-deckers in 1994, and a small coach hire business was bolstered by Mercedes minicoaches and a Leyland Leopard. A reasonable level of profitability was finally achieved in the mid-1990s, allowing a rapid expansion – forty-two vehicles were added to the fleet between 1993 and 1998. However, not all saw service and a number passed to Stagecoach in 1997 when most commercial bus routes were bought out by the owner of Western, A1 and AA. Towards the end of the decade the variety of vehicle types was increased by Dodge and Renault minibuses, Volvo Ailsa double-deckers, a solitary Leyland Olympian, the first of a number of Leyland Tigers, and an AEC Reliance bought as part of a job lot and which remains in the fleet as a rare operating example of this famous British marque. A batch of Leyland Nationals and our first Optare MetroRider completed the variety. Fifty-eight buses and coaches were purchased during the 1990s and the decade closed with the fleet standing at twenty-two vehicles.

G831RDS, a 20-seat Dormobile-bodied Ford Transit, on the Irvine to Kilwinning service in July 1990. Last-minute delivery of the first two vehicles meant they had to run in white for over a year. The first destination screens were specified to fit the preferred Carlyle-bodied Iveco bus and didn't fit the Transits properly – the Ivecos never materialised. (WMG)

831 is seen at Irvine Cross on 03/10/95 working a local service to Hunter Drive. This vehicle was later fitted with bus seats from a withdrawn Sherpa, and later still regained coach seats after local services passed to Stagecoach and the business concentrated on contracts and hires. (BN)

G832RDS was also a Dormobile Ford Transit, but a shorter 16-seater. In this very early view, it is at Broomlands Terminus, Irvine, on 21/02/90. The driver is a youthful David Granger, one of the founders and now the company's Managing Director. (AD)

832 was a very reliable vehicle and so was allocated to the subsidised service between Galston and Hamilton, which ran through a very rural area. It is seen in Hamilton bus station, May 1993. These were the days before mobile phones were universal and so a breakdown could mean a long walk for the driver! 832 was subsequently sold to Horsburgh, Pumpherston. (WMG)

D867NVS, a Carlyle-bodied Freight Rover Sherpa, is seen in Kilmarnock on the short-lived local service between Riccarton and the William Lows supermarket on 25/03/91. 867 saw further service in the town after sale to Neills Buses of Kilmarnock. (AD)

867 sits over the pit while under maintenance. This was the best of the early Sherpas, the Freight Rover mechanicals seemingly happier under the smaller 16-seater body, finding 20 seats a bit of a strain – it wasn't popular with drivers or passengers though. Note the Boyd's Handybus vehicle in the background – Boyds ran a couple of these unusual Salvador Caetano-bodied Ivecos 79.14s, but they did not stand up well to service work. (DG)

The first service in Kilmarnock was an immediate success, carrying full loads for much of the day, so Freight Rover Sherpa Dormobile F390OAS was pressed into service still wearing the colours of its first owner, Inverness Traction.

A repainted 390 is seen at Irvine Cross in April 1993 leading an AA Leyland National and an A1 Service Volvo B10M. Western vehicles in various liveries added to the colourful variety in Irvine at this time. This bus managed four years in the fleet despite its poor reliability before it was sold, together with 867, to Neills Buses. (WMG)

Aitken of Linlithgow only bodied seven minibuses and two came to us after their first owner, independent operator Inverness Traction, folded. Yet to gain fleetnames, F214NST is seen in the snow in Blacklands, Kilwinning, in 1990. (DG)

The two Aitken Sherpas are seen at the garage in 1991. Both buses were sold to and then bought back from Boyd's Handybus in 1993, then sold to Blythswood Motors and immediately leased back, and ended their eventful career with us when sold to Stark, Bridge of Weir. (DG)

F804NAS in Irvine during October 1991 with an AA Scania in close attendance. These vehicles suffered from poor ventilation and became very warm whenever the sun came out, meaning that they were equally unpopular with drivers and passengers. The mechanics weren't their greatest fans either, the Land Rover engine being particularly problematic. (MC)

804 has gained a yellow stripe and is seen at Irvine Cross on 07/07/93, pursued by Western's Leyland Leopard KL633 on service 14, which at that time ran from Kilmarnock to Beith. (BN)

The limitations of the first Sherpas led to the purchase of another new Dormobile Ford Transit, G188GSG, which operated the busy Wardneuk to Kilmarnock town centre service. Seen in Kilmarnock carrying an advert for the Metro nightclub, 22/02/94. Clyde Coast Coaches were also competing with Western in Kilmarnock at this time and one of their buses is seen in the background. (AD)

G188GSG at Irvine Cross on 06/03/95, sharing the stance with an AA Motor Services Leyland National. 188 was yet another vehicle eventually sold to Neills Buses. (BN)

A pair of unusual Talbot Pullman tri-axle minibuses were acquired from Canavan, Kilsyth, and E332LHG is seen at the garage shortly after its arrival in 1991. These vehicles suffered from poor reliability and did not stay in the fleet for long, 332 being sold to an operator in faraway Penzance. (DG)

E565MAC at Irvine Cross in 1991. The tri-axle arrangement did not work well on a bus, rear braking effort was poor and these buses could run a long way with a punctured rear tyre before the driver would notice, costing us a number of tyres. This vehicle ended up a bit closer to home, being sold to Roadrunner, Greenock.

The new order – almost new Dormobile Routemaker-bodied Mercedes 709D J607KGB leaves Irvine Cross heading for Kilwinning on 17/07/92. These buses combined many of the advantages of both minibuses and full-size vehicles and attracted significant numbers of passengers from our competitors. (AD)

Delivered in yellow and white, by October 1997 J609KGB had gained an overall advert for Specsavers, Irvine. The 709Ds were extremely reliable and required far less maintenance than the Transits, Sherpas and Talbots our mechanics were used to. These vehicles lost their work when a package of routes passed to Stagecoach and both were sold to McNairn, Coatbridge. (WMG)

Mechanically simple, the Transits were easy to maintain – we could change a clutch in 40 minutes flat. Dormobile Ford Transit F979EDS was the first of four similar vehicles bought second-hand between 1991 and 1994 and is seen in the sun at Irvine Cross on 15/05/95. 979 came from Peter Harte, Greenock. (BN)

Carlyle-bodied Freight Rover Sherpa D859KWR was bought from Boyd's in 1993 and is seen at Irvine Cross in March 1995. Sisters D858KWR and D866LWR arrived at the same time but 858 was broken for spares and 866 sold to Neills Buses, Kilmarnock, without either being used. (WMG)

New to London Transport as OJD11R, ECW-bodied Bristol LHS6L WGD901R had done the rounds of Ayrshire operators having served with Keenans of Coalhall, AD Coaches of Dundonald, and Boyd's Handybus. We bought it for tendered service 339, which ran between Kilwinning station and Irvine station via Benslie, the 28 seats being needed on a peak journey serving a school. It lasted less than a year and was sold to Ash, High Wycombe, via ADT Auctions in Manchester. (DG)

The replacement vehicle for service 339 in 1993 was Bedford YMQ WNH51W, also ex-Boyd's, which had a rare – and fairly utilitarian – Lex Maxeta body. This bus was popular with the drivers as it had an automatic gearbox and heaters, both of which the Bristol lacked. Seen here at Irvine Cross in May 1995, it ended its days in our yard as a barrier against stone-throwing children and was broken up on site. (WMG)

G734PGA was a Mercedes 814D from another Greenock operator, Caldwell Coaches. It boasted high-back seats and a boot to improve the minicoach hire offering, but it was equally at home on local services despite having a narrow entrance and lacking destination gear. Seen here at Irvine Cross on 07/07/93 with Western Fleetline KR855. This vehicle possessed a mean turn of speed. It later gained the dateless registration HXI733, but structural problems resulted in it being traded in for K770AFS. (BN)

Another dual-purpose vehicle acquired in 1993 was Dormobile Ford Transit G443ETW from Wayland's Coaches in Beccles, Norfolk. Here it is at Irvine Cross in July 1993 heading for Kilwinning with a competing AA National close behind. The driver of the Transit is Willie Neil and the pedestrian is David Lockie, both of whom were directors of Shuttle Buses at the time. 443 was sold to a former employee based in Galston who was starting out in business for himself. (BN)

Following the success of the first two Dormobile-bodied Mercedes 709Ds a third entered service in 1993 as L917UGA, seen here at the garage between duties when nearly new. Despite the relatively high floor, the wide bodies and large windows of these buses offered passengers a much more pleasant journey than the Transits and Sherpas. (DG)

The following year L698AGA, a Mercedes 811D with bodywork by Wadham Stringer, joined the fleet. Persistent engine problems meant its stay in the fleet was a short one. Pictured here at Irvine Cross on 07/09/94, it was sold to an operator in Wiltshire. (BN)

NLE515 was an AEC Regal IV new to London Transport in 1953. It was bought from the family living in it in a field near Newton Stewart in 1992. Here it is being prepared for the chassis to be shot-blasted, an activity which did not please the local council when they got to hear about it. (DG)

Unfortunately the restoration was never completed despite considerable time and money being expended. The bus was resold to a preservationist in Shefford, Bedfordshire, several years later. Its subsequent fate is unknown. (DG)

Our first double-decker was Leyland Fleetline FE30AGR OUC48R, also ex-London Transport as their DMS2048. We acquired it from local operator Kerr's of Galston in 1994. Presumably this bus had power steering and some form of suspension earlier in its life, but neither was much in evidence by the time it got to us. Here it is operating service 339 in 1995 with another former LT bus in the background, a Titan drafted in by Stagecoach to replace unserviceable A1 vehicles. (WMG)

A much nicer DMS was THX642S, a Leyland Fleetline FE30ALR with Park Royal body bought from one of the Barnsley scrapyards in 1995. LT had upgraded this to B20 specification, including fitting an Iveco engine more usually found in marine applications. Seen here in Irvine on 29/05/97 operating a commercial school service to Marr College in Troon, this vehicle gave us eight years' service before sale to a preservationist. (AD)

D40UAO was the first of a series of smaller Mercedes L608D minibuses bought from Stagecoach Western in 1994. It carried Reeve Burgess bodywork. (DG)

Its fleet livery soon reverted to Stagecoach stripes when we entered into a route-sharing agreement on the Wardneuk to Kilmarnock town centre service, where we operated as part of the Stagecoach network in the town but kept the farebox revenue. Later this vehicle was returned to fleet livery and re-registered VJI3001, although it ran for nearly a year registered UJI3001 before the mistake was noticed. (DG)

PGA 829V was a Leyland Leopard PSU3F/4R Alexander AT unique in the Western fleet, all their other T-types being on Seddon Pennine chassis. Re-registered DAZ8290 this became our first full-size private hire coach in 1994, although it spent much of its time working school contracts and occasionally appeared on service 339. (DG)

The first minicoach bought solely for private hire work was Robin Hood-bodied 811D F88GGC, seen here in Paisley on 03/07/99. New to R&I Tours of London, it had an automatic gearbox giving very jerky gearchanges, which was replaced with a manual. This vehicle was re-registered VJI3001 after the L608D pictured on page 22 was sold, and gave us a long life before it was sold for export. (BN)

E689WKJ was another Dormobile-bodied Ford Transit, pictured here in Irvine on 15/05/95. It stood out from its sisters by virtue of its black painted windscreen surround. It came that way and we liked it, so it stayed. It passed on to TJ Walsh of Halifax. (BN)

N2SBL was an Alexander Sprint-bodied Mercedes 709D delivered in 1996 wearing blue and white and Neills Buses fleetnames. When Billy Neill decided to retire, Stagecoach wanted his very profitable route between Kilmarnock and Kilmaurs but didn't want to be seen to be increasing their near-monopoly of services in the area. Consequently, we bought this bus, took over Neills' route, ran it for six months while Stagecoach stayed out of our way, and then de-registered it. (DG)

Two buses were needed to maintain Neills' service and so we also bought Freight Rover Sherpa F211AKD and painted it accordingly. It did see occasional service on our own school contracts. (DG)

When the time came to hand Neills' service over to Stagecoach in 1997, N2SBL was repainted into fleet livery and put to work from Kilwinning. Here it is at Irvine Cross on 26/08/97. This bus was sold to Stagecoach in 1997 along with most of our local services but remained working the Kilwinning local service and often returned to our garage whilst the driver took his lunch break. (BN)

C602NPU, a Carlyle-bodied Ford Transit, had a brief stay in the fleet between 1996 and 1997 before being sold to Gordon, Southwaite. Pictured on a contract in Kilmarnock, August 1996. (WMG)

E644DCK was the first of a number of Dodge and Renault S56s, arriving in 1996 from the A1 Service fleet of Stagecoach. It was yet another Dormobile-bodied member of the fleet. It is seen at Irvine Cross heading for Kilwinning on 24/08/96. (MC)

644 later became another vehicle carrying an overall advert for Specsavers, Irvine. (DG)

K770AFS, a Plaxton-bodied Mercedes 814D, was another upgrade to the private hire fleet in 1996 when it replaced 733. Seen here on a school trip at Kelvingrove Art Gallery, Glasgow, on 06/06/97. We discovered that 33 seats was a very popular size for school hires, accommodating a standard class of 30 with the requisite three teachers. (BN)

770 was a one of number of buses that carried all-over adverts for the Grange Bingo in Stevenston, for which we operated a number of contract routes. It gave eleven years' service and was then sold to local operator Bennetts of Kilwinning. (DG)

G737PGA was the seventh and final Dormobile Ford Transit, arriving in 1994 from local operator Wynter-M of Irvine. Most of these vehicles were eventually sold to TJ Walsh of Halifax, another fan of the Transit. The business unfortunately closed in 2020 as a result of the COVID-19 pandemic. (SB)

Probably the best service buses we operated (back in the days when step entrances were acceptable) were J216XKY and J217XKY, Alexander Sprint 25-seater Mercedes 709Ds that came from Reg's of Hertford in 1995. 216 is seen part-way through a repaint before work started on 217. (DG)

The finished product at Irvine Cross, 06/08/96. These buses were easy to maintain and highly manoeuvrable; the lightweight, mainly aluminium bodies meant they had better fuel consumption than the longer and heavier Dormobile 709Ds. (BN)

Sister J217XKY, also at Irvine Cross on the same date. Both were sold to Stagecoach along with our local services in 1997 but remained in Ayrshire, often on our former routes and driven by our former drivers, but now carrying Stagecoach stripes. (BN)

Another unique vehicle in the fleet was HIL 3188, a Leyland Olympian with East Lancs coach spec bodywork, branded the 'Super Shuttle'. This coach had a TL11 engine and apparently no speed limiter as it would cruise at 80 mph effortlessly. It was fitted with seatbelts in the company's workshops but another financial crisis (and its eye-watering fuel consumption) resulted in its sale to Eastville Coaches of Bristol. (DG)

Two very dilapidated Mercedes 709D Dormobile 29-seaters, H124YGG and H667AGD, were acquired from Bridge, Paisley, in 1997 and refurbished by the company. The level of rebuilding necessary is evident in this picture of 667, taken on 27/04/97. (AD)

H124YGG was re-registered IUI9892 and gave another ten years' service. It carried a variety of advertising liveries including the Grange Bingo, seen previously on K770AFS, and this one for the XS Stock Shop, Irvine, pictured at Irvine Cross working service 13 to Stewarton in August 2003. (WMG)

H667AGD was similarly re-registered IUI3467 but served for less than two years before sale to Rooney, Newry. Fresh from the paintshop, it is working the Hunter Drive service in June 1997. (WMG)

D238URG was a coach-seated 16-seater Alexander AM-bodied Mercedes L608D previously with The Minibus Company of Edinburgh, sharing yard space with pioneer 831 in July 1999. (WMG)

Less fortunate was similar D99VVC, bought from Arriva for spares in 1998.

C417VVN was another L608D, previously with East Yorkshire Motor Services but carrying the remains of an overall advert for the Samaritans. This bus did not stay in the fleet for long and was never repainted. Its paintwork did not present a good image for the company and so it did not carry fleet names. Seen on the A78 near Irvine in March 1999. (WMG)

A pair of modern double-deckers arrived in 1998, OSN851Y direct from Tayside, Dundee, and OSN860Y originally from the same source but via a Merseyside operator. Both were Volvo Ailsa B55-10 Mk IIIs built in Irvine less than a mile from our garage and fitted with Northern Counties bodywork. (DG)

The high-capacity 86-seater buses were fitted with tachographs and were very popular for school trips. 851 is seen on a private hire at Nuneaton Street, Glasgow, 16/10/99. (BN)

860 at the garage in July 1999, prior to operating the free service from Irvine to Blackshaw Farm Park near West Kilbride. The drivers loved these buses in the winter when heat from the front-mounted engine kept the cab warm. They were less popular in the summer for the same reason. (WMG)

A second Dodge S56 was E634DCK from Goosecroft, Denny, looking a bit down at heel at the garage in 1999. (DG)

634 and 644 were sold to Houston Ramm in 2000, part-exchanged for a pair of Optare MetroRiders – one of which is seen on the left. (DG)

E346WYS was another S56 but this time badged as a Renault and fitted with an Alexander AM body. New to Clydeside Scottish, this arrived from Hall, Kennoway, as a part exchange in 1998. Originally intended for spares only, its heritage saw much time, effort and money expended to return it to service – David Granger had worked for Clydeside from June 1985 to August 1986. It was sold to a preservationist in Paisley in 2001. (DG)

Never afraid to try something new, as long as it was cheap, Leyland Nationals started arriving in 1998 including OJD888R from Mike Nash Bus Sales of Cobham. Bought for school work, it is seen here in the yard in March 1999 sandwiched between an Ailsa and a Fleetline. It retained its red London Transport livery until sold for conversion into a Sky TV hospitality unit. (WMG)

JTU593T was a National from the strangely named Optional Bus of Leeds in 1998. It was only briefly used and was never repainted. Most of our Nationals had the fixed head 500 engine, which was notorious for leaking oil and blowing smoke. Ours were no exception. (WMG)

593 ended its days along with another National as a barricade to stop children throwing stones through the yard fence. It was broken up on site – the scrapman was astonished by how hard it was to dismantle, but the bodies always were the best part of the National. (DG)

GSU551, a Plaxton Paramount 3500-bodied Leyland Tiger, came from Viscount Central of Burnley in 1998 as the Tiger became the standard fleet coach – they were much cheaper than the equivalent Volvo! Seen on the A78 near Irvine in March 1999. (WMG)

551 on a school trip at the Odeon Cinema, Kilmarnock on 27/03/03, now in full fleet livery. The cherished registration was supposed to have been returned to Viscount Central and the coach re-registered A201MFR, but they closed down before the transfer was completed and the plate remains owned today. (AD)

No fewer than twelve vehicles joined the fleet in 1998, including this 16-seater Ford Transit, L157PKU. (WMG)

Probably the most famous vehicle owned by the company, and still an active member of the fleet, is Plaxton Supreme 53-seater AEC Reliance, bought unseen as a job lot along with OSN860R and GSU551. It is pictured in the yard in August 1999 having acquired dateless registration 875YYA. (AD)

Enthusiast, and driver for Shuttle Buses, Lawrence Macduff has been instrumental in keeping the Reliance on the road and looking its best. Here it is on an enthusiasts' tour on board the MV *Loch Dunvegan* on 05/07/08. (LM)

A major structural failure almost led to the vehicle's demise but a full restoration was undertaken between 2012 and 2016 when the coach regained its age-appropriate registration. Seen here at at the Scottish Vintage Bus Museum at Lathalmond carrying Shuttle Coaches branding. (LM)

Another National was NIL7242, which came from Dart Buses of Paisley in 1999. Unlike its predecessors it did gain fleet livery, and served for a creditable five years. July 2002. (WMG)

Buy One Get One Free is nothing new – NIL7241 arrived from Dart at the same time as a source of spares. (WMG)

The final double-decker acquired (so far) was Leyland Atlantean AN68 Alexander AL UJI8218. This came from Economic, a low-cost operating unit of Busways in Newcastle, in 1996 as SCN271S. It is seen here in Largs returning from a school run to Skelmlorlie. This was a lovely bus to drive but constant problems with gearbox leaks led to its sale to a breaker. (SB)

WJI9367 was another Leyland National from Dart Buses and was the final National bought before seatbelts became mandatory on school buses. (DG)

Another bus bought for spares was Dodge S56 D921KWW from First Stop, Renfrew. The back of a rare CVE Omni minibus can be seen on the left – several of these vehicles were maintained on behalf of local nursing homes for a while, but they proved chronically unreliable. (WMG)

The mid-90s wasn't a great era for vehicle presentation; the external condition of Ford Transit school bus C89AUB generated a lot of adverse comments from parents and it was moved on very quickly.

Two more Leyland Tigers arrived in 1999. A121GSA, which had a rather utilitarian Alexander P-type body, came to us from Stagecoach Bluebird. It is seen on a school hire at the Odeon, Kilmarnock, on 27/03/03. (AD)

The second Tiger to arrive in 1999, B149LAG, carried a much more stylish Duple Laser 2 body. By the time it was pictured here at Glasgow's Kelvin Hall in March 2002 it had acquired the registration WJI9367 from the National pictured on page 43. (BN)

Shortly before step-entrance buses were swept away by the low-floor revolution, the final version of Optare's MetroRider appeared in the fleet in 1999 when MR17 S310KNW was bought new for a tendered service between Dundonald and Ayr. This vehicle spent its entire working life with the company, clocking up thirteen years' service before it was sold for scrap. Pictured in Prestwick, May 2001. (WMG)

The 2000s

The MetroRider was the first new bus bought for several years and marked the start of a major improvement in the quality of the fleet, both buses and coaches. Vehicles were now bought for life, not just out of short-term necessity, and many acquisitions around this time went on to have extremely long lives with the company.

More used MetroRiders arrived, but a change of policy saw examples of the virtually indestructible Plaxton Beaver Mercedes O.814 Vario join the service bus fleet. Investment was made in several midicoaches to bolster the private hire fleet, and a number of new minibuses arrived – predominantly for school work but available for hires in the evenings and at weekends.

The low-floor revolution saw the arrival of the first truly accessible buses. Initially these were second-hand examples, but the highlight of the decade came in 2006 when we achieved the distinction of becoming the first Scottish operator to take delivery of the new Alexander Dennis Enviro 200. SN56AYF and AYG were presented to us at ADL's factory in Falkirk followed by lunch in the boardroom and a photoshoot at Airth Castle – and at a stroke we had made the transition from upstart independent to part of the establishment.

After this brief flirtation with Alexander Dennis, who appeared to be more interested in the big groups ordering buses by the dozen rather than companies like us who ordered in ones and twos, Optare became the supplier of choice and the first of many Solos joined the fleet.

Houston Ramm, our principal used vehicle supplier, went spectacularly bust but not before dropping several turkeys on us. Replacement vehicle suppliers were found in the shape of Jim Stones, a renowned high-quality independent operator in Leigh, and Dawsonrentals, who provided a number of more modern coaches to replace the Tigers. Dawsonrentals offered a rent-to-buy scheme (which required little cash up front but a lot over the following years) and three Caetano-bodied coaches, two Dennis Javelins and a Volvo B10M, were acquired this way.

This decade saw us branching out into SPT's MyBus Demand Responsive services, an operation which has since grown to become the foundation of the business. After we built up a small fleet of Solos to operate DRT routes, SPT began providing their own vehicles to go with their contracts towards the end of the decade. The first new SPT buses were an Optare Solo and two VW Bluebird Tucanas – things were looking promising, but this was the calm before the storm.

The thirty-seven vehicles which arrived during the 2000s was almost matched by the number of departures, meaning that the fleet strength had only increased by five to twenty-seven at the end of the decade.

The need to replace the Dodges with something more modern, coupled with the success of the first MetroRider, led to three more arriving in close succession. J934JJR was an MR03 from Go-Ahead North East via Houston Ramm, who took Dodges 634 and 644 in part exchange. It is seen here freshly painted at the garage in July 2000. (WMG)

The same bus but with a new livery and a new registration, AHZ7308 is on a private hire in Carmichael Street, Glasgow, on 27/04/02. (BN)

For several years we operated journeys on service 361 between Ayr, Straiton and Dunure. J939JJR had been re-registered AHZ7309 by March 2001 and is seen here at Boswell Park in Ayr on 17/09/01. These two buses proved very reliable, which was fortunate as the 361 took them deep into rural South Ayrshire and a long way from Kilwinning. (BN)

Six months later and 309 has succumbed to the Grange Bingo overall advert. Both these buses had seatbelts and tachographs and were regularly used on private hire work; beneath threatening skies, this is a school trip to Glasgow Science Centre on 18/03/02. (BN)

Strathclyde Partnership for Transport began offering grants to upgrade vehicles used on their subsidised local services and advantage was taken to replace the Mercedes 608D used on service 332, which ran from Kilmarnock via Fenwick and Moscow (the one in Ayrshire, not the Russian one) to Galston. X311ABU was an O.814 Vario with a Plaxton Beaver 2 body, a terrific combination. (DG)

By March 2003 311 had gained XS Stock Shop livery but was still working on the 332. It was soon transferred onto the demanding service 13, running between Irvine and Stewarton for many years before being sold for scrap in 2018 having run three quarters of a million miles. The reliability of the Vario was legendary, and the original engine from 311 is still in service today, powering Solo N6SBL. (AD)

Another long-lived vehicle was Mayflower conversion Ford Transit S515GGD, which was previously a non-PSV rental vehicle with TLS, Salford. We got an extraordinary further fourteen years' life out of this bus, admittedly with a huge rebuild part way through that involved renewal of the entire floor. Not an easy job. (DG)

The first Metrorider proved a supremely reliable bus and so was joined by another MR17, S904DUB, from Wilsons of Rhu in 2001. Both buses ran until 2013 when their age, and impending low-floor legislation, saw them sold for scrap to bus breakers Dunsmore of Larkhall. 904 is seen in Kilmarnock in April 2008 with the landmark railway arches in the background. (WMG)

The success of the first Vario led to the acquisition of similar T294ROF from Jim Stones, Leigh, seen here in December 2003 at Irvine heading for Stewarton on service 13. Visible in the background are a Stagecoach A1 service double-decker, a Stagecoach AA single-decker, and a First Dennis Dart that was part of a short-lived incursion into Ayrshire by FirstGroup. (WMG)

An Alexander TC-bodied Leyland Tiger arrived from Dochertys of Irvine registered GSU342, later regaining its original B208FFS. It stayed with us for fifteen years, latterly only licensed in May and June for the busy season of school summer outings, and was sold for preservation in Fife in 2019. Halfway through its life with the company, it is operating a rail replacement journey from Largs to Kilwinning here at Ardrossan, driven by Lawrence Macduff. (DG)

Service 31 ran deep into Stagecoach territory between West Kilbride and Irvine. When we decided to speed it up as the X31 and convert it to low-floor operation we turned to Jim Stones again. Dennis Dart SLF Plaxton Pointer MPD T337TVM was one of two MPDs that came north. Saltcoats, November 2003. (WMG)

A hugely significant event was the 2004 removal of HAD Coaches from SPT's Dial-A-Bus services in the Kilmarnock area. Since we were one of the few local operators who ran low-floor buses we were immediately drafted in as HAD's replacement and 337 is entering Kilmarnock bus station in June of that year. The X31 reverted to step-entrance buses until we were able to hire in suitable replacement vehicles for the Dial-A-Bus services. (WMG)

By now the company was carving out a niche in the lucrative minicoach private hire market. T56RJL was another Mercedes O.814 Vario, this time with an Autobus Classique Nouvelle 2 coach body. Like most of the vehicles bought around this time, it gave excellent service, running for ten years. Seen on a private hire in Kilmarnock, in August 2002. (WMG)

Our first Scania was G757SRB, an N113 from City of Nottingham in 2002, with the softened Alexander PS body. This was a nice bus to drive, easily maintained and very reliable, but despite this the next Scanias wouldn't arrive for another seventeen years. It spent most of its life on rail replacement and school duties, as here in Saltcoats in October 2004. (WMG)

The second Dennis Dart MPD from Jim Stones was T902JTD. Despite carrying route branding for the X31, it is arriving at Irvine from Stewarton on service 113 in May 1997. (WMG)

A batch of new school contracts in 2004 led to the arrival of three new dual-purpose minibuses. SJ04FLA, a Mercedes 614D Vario, was the first, and was used on private hire work at the weekends as here in Hope Street, Glasgow, on 08/04/07. Despite the propensity of these Onyx van-derived bodies to rust, this bus is still in the fleet in 2020, now registered 875YYA. (BN)

When the Dial-A-Bus contracts were retained on five-year contracts in the summer of 2004 a batch of three new M850 Solos arrived as YJ54ZXU, ZXV and ZXW. ZXU immediately became N5SBL, the mark chosen to denote ownership by Shuttle Buses Limited, as these buses carried SPT livery with no reference to the operator except the miniscule legal lettering. Kilmarnock, April 2008. (WMG)

YJ54ZXV became N6SBL and is in Kilmarnock on its usual Dial-A-Bus service in August 2008. N6SBL and N7SBL regained their original registrations and were sold to Llew Jones, Llanrwst, in 2011 when SPT began providing their own vehicles for Dial-A-Bus contracts. (WMG)

N7SBL was delivered as YJ54ZXW and spent its entire life working Dial-A-Bus service M1, covering rural East Ayrshire. It is pictured here in July 2005 in Ayr with the regular driver collecting a passenger in a wheelchair. This bus was involved in a serious accident when nearly new and spent six months back at Optare while the front end was extensively rebuilt. (WMG)

Another Dennis Dart came from Houston Ramm as a back-up to the first two, although J383GKH was an older step-entrance model. When it arrived, the engine and gearbox were on their last legs and had to be replaced before the bus entered service. Pictured at Irvine Cross in July 2005 on the West Kilbride service. (WMG)

383, pictured above, was one of a trio of buses arriving from Rochdale. The second was MetroRider L384YFT, carrying this appropriate destination. It looked good on top but was rotten underneath and was dismantled for spares, never entering service. Houston Ramm had agreed to take it back for a refund but the transaction was not completed before he went bust. (DG)

Another new bus for the 2004 school contracts was SF54CHK, a Mercedes 311 Sprinter. It was on a private hire in Glasgow on 20/03/05. (BN)

When our AEC Reliance suffered engine failure in 2004, we were fortunate to be offered JGE346T, a preservation project that had literally fallen apart due to body corrosion. Part-owned by our driver Lawrence Macduff, it is seen here next to Lawrence's MacBraynes Reliance. We removed many useful parts from 346 and the remains were broken up at our garage. (LM)

SPT continued to part-fund vehicle improvements. Optare Solo M920 N3SBL was a 33-seater that arrived in 2005 wearing SPT livery. It is seen in a wet Saltcoats on 26/11/07, by which time it had been repainted into fleet colours. (AD)

The third new school bus was another Mercedes Sprinter, SF05AKK, seen here with its sister when new. The two Sprinters spent their entire lives with the company before going for scrap to local dealer Barry Devlin Services at Knockentiber in 2018. (DG)

We needed another low-floor bus as backup for the two MPDs and Stuarts of Carluke provided X704UKS. It broke down on its delivery run and things didn't get a lot better over the next two years. Its unreliability was in stark contrast to the MPDs bought from Jim Stones and was a lesson for us in the importance of preventative maintenance for modern, relatively complicated buses. (DG)

The third and final new vehicle part-funded by SPT was a 29-seater M850 Solo, which was given the N2SBL registration from the departed Mercedes. It carries SPT livery and route branding for the Irvine to Stewarton service that it is operating in typical Ayrshire autumn weather on 26/11/07. (AD)

N590GBW was acquired from Dawsonrentals and was the first Dennis Javelin GX in the fleet with a stylish (for the time) Caetano Algarve 2 body. It had been upseated to 70 seats for work as a school bus but was found working wedding hires most weekends despite the very close spacing of the seats – 70 adults crammed onto this bus was a claustrophobic experience. (LM)

Another Algarve 2, but this time on a Volvo B10M-60 chassis, K708RNR was quickly re-registered GSU342. It is being anxiously marshalled off the Largs ferry at Cumbrae Slip on 12/06/11. (LM)

Pictures of the second Autobus Classique Nouvelle 2 Mercedes O.814, W603KFE, are rare. A few months after its arrival it was caught up in a workshop fire whilst under maintenance at our local Mercedes dealership, Caledonian Trucks in Ayr, and was totally destroyed. (DG)

The highlight of this decade was undoubtedly the arrival in 2006 of the first two ADL Enviro 200s for any Scottish operator, SN56AYF and AYG. AYF is picking up at Saltcoats Station on service X31 for Irvine on 26/11/07. (AD)

Sister AYG, also at Saltcoats but heading towards West Kilbride, attracts an envious glance from a Stagecoach driver. Both E200s were to sold to Stagecoach in 2009 along with most local services. (DG)

The Algarve 2 was the preferred body in the mid-1990s and another two followed the first. M721LJR from Dawsonrentals was a Volvo B10M-62, quickly re-registered GSU551. On 15/06/12 it was awaiting a party coming off the Arran ferry at Ardrossan. (LM)

The second Optare Solo to carry N7SBL arrived in 2007 as YE52FHD. It had coach seats, belts and a tachograph, and carved out a market for group hires where an accessible bus was needed, but spends most of its time on service work and is currently the allocated vehicle for the Largs local service. It is seen here on park and ride work at Turnberry with N2SBL, 29/07/12. (LM)

SF05FNZ is a Plaxton Cheetah Mercedes O.814 Vario, seen here surrounded by Lothian buses in Edinburgh's Princes Street in September 2007, shortly after acquisition from Mitchell, Plean. (WMG)

This vehicle, along with sister SF06FSO, was given a full refurbishment in 2016 and rebranded in Shuttle Coaches livery. By now it carried fleet number 1 and so gained dateless registration TJZ1001. It was on a school run near Ardrossan on 26/04/17. (RK)

The fourth, and last, Algarve 2 was M786VJO, another Dennis Javelin, which became GSU142. It is seen here at Grange Academy, Kilmarnock, on 20/04/17. 551 and 142 each gave thirteen years' service before being sold for scrap in 2019. (LM)

Just one vehicle arrived in 2008. L746LWA was a Mercedes 709D, purchased along with the business of the Thistle Bus Company, which ran the Dalry local service. The bus was unroadworthy on arrival and sold for scrap without being operated. Thistle was the successor to the Valley Bus Co., infamous for being caught by VOSA with a portable Calor gas heater warming one of their buses. We operated the Dalry local service until 2019, when it was given up as passenger numbers declined. (DG)

In a significant change of policy which would have major implications for us, SPT began supplying the buses for some new Dial-A-Bus contracts. YX09HRF and HRG were the first, a pair of Bluebird Tucanas based on a VW T5 chassis cab. Arriving in a very dull maroon SPT livery, they were quickly repainted orange when the service was rebranded as MyBus. HRF was shared between us and the British Red Cross, who operated the DRT contract on Arran, and it is seen at Brodick on 07/11/10. (LM)

The Tucanas were a lightweight design and therefore unsuitable for some of the more arduous MyBus routes. Consequently, Optare Solo YJ09OUP was provided by SPT for service M1. Half a million miles later it remains in the fleet in 2020 and is now owned by the company. (DG)

The 2010s

After the rather unstructured vehicle purchasing policies of the first twenty years a degree of uniformity began to pervade the local bus service fleet, although vehicles for MyBus and private hire work continued to come from a variety of builders and brought yet more diversity into the fleet.

The early potential of SPT's Tucanas was not fulfilled, with suspension, doors and gearboxes proving especially problematic. The first batch was quickly replaced with updated examples that were slightly more reliable but SPT went completely off the wall next, buying a large number of unproven vehicles based on Renault running units, put together in Italy and finished off in Glasgow. Despite coming to us new, the Car-Ind LoBus was the worst designed and most unreliable bus we have ever operated – and we've bought more than a few lemons over the years. Fortunately, SPT eventually abandoned the LoBus project and went back to Bluebird for their Fiat-based Orion minibus, though this was another design not without its faults. Finally sense prevailed and they started to provide Optare Solos for DRT contracts before making another U-turn and reverting to operator-supplied vehicles after a very unhappy (and expensive) seven years for all concerned.

Freed from the need to invest in the MyBus fleet, we added further new and nearly-new vehicles to the school and private hire fleet bringing KingLong and MAN chassis for the first time, along with more modern Volvos. Having disposed of most our Tigers some years previously, the arrival of two ex-Ulsterbus examples was a bit of a step back in time. The first new midicoaches were bought in 2013 and 2017, both with Turas bodywork built in Portugal. Our first 15m coach was a tri-axle Volvo from Megabus, and more tri-axles followed when two repossessed Irizar PB Scanias were bought from a finance company, one being an ex-England football team coach. Many vehicles were rebranded into Shuttle Coaches livery, initially white with a yellow flash but later with a more elaborate design.

Local service work and MyBus contract work increased once again meaning that more second-hand Solos were required. The big manufacturers seemed to take notice of us now, and a host of demonstrators were provided by a variety of builders and used extensively on local service and MyBus work. We were not sufficiently impressed by any of the competition to move away from Optare, and three new Solos along with one nearly-new example joined the fleet between 2012 and 2017.

However, rising prices and lengthening delivery dates from Optare led to a significant change in our purchasing policy in 2018 when the first new Mercedes Sprinter-based Mellor Strata was purchased followed by seven more in 2019. These were the first low-carbon vehicles in the fleet, benefitting from good fuel consumption and qualifying for a higher rate of Bus Service Operator's Grant. The £570,000 order for six Stratas placed in June 2019 was the largest in the company's history.

No fewer than sixty buses and coaches were added to the fleet in this decade. There were some disposals, but at the end of 2019 fleet strength stood at an all-time high of fifty-five.

The two 2009 Tucanas were nowhere near robust enough for MyBus duties and were quickly replaced by five later examples, YX59DZB, YX10AXM, AXN, AXR and AXS, as more contracts changed to SPT-provided buses. Unusually, AXN was found on service work on 29/05/11 operating short workings on service 29 from Irvine Cross to Montgomerie Park due to a road closure. (LM)

Even these upgraded Tucanas had their fair share of problems, and AXM is seen in distress in Kilmarnock on 02/04/13. (LM)

A second Plaxton Cheetah arrived as SF06FSO. On 16/09/10 it is pictured in Glasgow – parked in the fast lane between junctions 1 and 2 of the M77! The event was the papal visit at nearby Bellahouston Park, with the motorway used as a coach park. (LM)

Following refurbishment and rebranding, it is now fleet no. 11, registered TJZ1011. Seen on school duties at Greenwood Academy, Dreghorn. (LM)

For the next round of MyBus vehicles SPT imported a batch of CarInd LoBuses from Italy, based on Renault Master running units. We were given two, SF10GKC and GKD. They were a total disaster from day one. The yellow jackets seen inside GKC are mechanics carrying out warranty work, an almost daily occurrence at times. (MC)

We wrestled with the LoBuses for nearly two years before SPT gave up on the project – we got about 15,000 miles a year out of each, well under half what a typical MyBus vehicle should achieve. Pictures of them on the move are therefore rare, but GKD was caught in Irvine High Street when nearly new. When they were actually in service, a particular problem was the front wheel drive with most of the weight over the rear axle. The result was a frightening appetite for tyres. (DD)

When the 2009 Tucanas were replaced, YX10AXF became the float vehicle between ourselves and the Red Cross on Arran. Here it is at Brodick on 13/01/16. This bus eventually passed into our ownership and is now the only Tucana remaining in service. (LM)

More Solos flooded into the fleet in the early part of the decade. First was CU06AWG, seen here working service 334 in Kilmarnock on 20/08/15. This was the first Solo not to carry an SBL registration. (LM)

The hire fleet was bolstered by the arrival of another 24-seater Onyx Mercedes, SF06FSS. Despite the identical appearance to SJ04FLA this is an O.814D. It was subsequently rebranded into Shuttle Coaches livery and was on a hire at the Riverside Museum in Glasgow on 24/06/18. (BN)

Providing a more modern image for the larger coaches, but sticking with Caetano bodywork, SM06SUN is a Volvo B12B carrying the Enigma body, bought from Simpsons of Rosehearty. It was re-registered SBL77 but ran in Simpson's blue and silver livery for several years before repaint, hence the rather incongruous blue fleetname seen here in Dunoon on 09/06/17. It is being overtaken by a West Coast Motors MCV-bodied Volvo B8R. (LM)

The first new Solo purchased for six years was SR YJ62FXZ, which had a wood-effect floor and e-leather seats for a relaunch of service 113. It keeps company with Stagecoach MAN 24189 at the terminus in Stewarton on 02/10/12. (LM)

Used Solos were arriving too – short versions YJ59PKF and PKO came from CumfyBus, Southport, via Optare, who had unusually taken them as trade-ins. PKF works service 38 to Kilwinning at Irvine Cross on 23/08/19, followed by a newer SR Solo working service 21 to Irvine Harbourside. (MC)

Sister YJ59PKO was working the lengthy service 337, which runs from Kilmarnock to Beith via a roundabout, rural route on 06/08/13. Here it sets off from Kilmarnock bus station under the watchful eye of the Stagecoach banksman. (LM)

The second Caetano Enigma was Volvo B12M FJ03VND that was re-registered SBL340. On 22/06/14 it was aboard the MV *Bute* heading for a tour of Argyll. (LM)

New emission regulations were about to kill off the Mercedes Vario and so we snapped up one of the last built. Turas-bodied O.818 YS13AAN was on a private hire at the Ormidale Estate near Glendaruel in Argyll on 06/06/14. (LM)

Plaxton's Beaver body returned to the fleet when Mercedes Vario O.814 PF51KHB was bought for a school contract. This vehicle remains in the fleet but has not seen use for several years. (RK)

School work also saw the arrival of three Alexander Belfast Leyland Tigers from Dodds of Troon, but new to Ulsterbus. PXI5515 was bought for spares and quickly broken up but PXI5517 put in five years' service before being sold to a preservationist in Northern Ireland. On 19/03/14 it is parked on the A71 near Kilmarnock with a Shuttle Buses Bluebird Orion about to pass. (LM)

The fate of PXI5523 was less fortunate – it went for scrap and finished up at Kilmarnock fire station being used as a training vehicle by the Scottish Fire and Rescue Service. (DG)

The fleet of SPT-owned Bluebird Tucanas needed bolstering and some spare capacity came when we bought a former Bluebird demonstrator, KX58BJF, which is chasing one of our Solos past Kilmarnock bus station on 06/08/13. (LM)

Supposedly a more appropriate offering from Bluebird for MyBus work was the Orion, based on Fiat Ducato running units, YX11CVM being our first. Five of these buses have been operated, some initially leased from SPT but all ultimately coming into our ownership. (DG)

Orion YX13BWC is seen on MyBus service M22 awaiting a passenger coming off the Arran ferry at Ardrossan ferry terminal on 16/06/14. We are currently SPT's largest contractor on the MyBus network, running sixteen services across Ayrshire, Renfrewshire and Glasgow. (LM)

Additional school contracts in 2014 required high-capacity vehicles. A Javelin was traded in for this KingLong XMQ6130C 73-seater, BX14KPG. It is seen at Irvine Harbour when new on 27/08/14, before fleetnames were applied. Our experience has been that KingLong is a decent product – the Cummins engines are built in Darlington, not China – let down by poor dealer support. (LM)

While an improvement on the Tucana, certainly in terms of passenger comfort, the Orions share some of the Tucana's faults, particularly suspensions and a troublesome automated gearbox. YX12CFZ was leased by SPT to McGills and we bought it for spares at the end of its lease in 2017. However, as it was virtually intact, we overhauled it and it is seen leaving Kilmarnock bus station on 03/09/18. (BN)

The ideal MyBus vehicle in our opinion – a short 7.1m Optare Solo. YD63VFB was owned by SPT when delivered in 2013, later passing into the company's ownership. It is used almost exclusively on the demanding M1 rural East Ayrshire MyBus service, as here in Ayr on 27/07/18. (BN)

PO11HVW and HVX are a pair of MAN A91 Beulas Stergo E 70-seater coaches. Despite their consecutive registrations they reached us from different sources – HVX was the first arrival, from its original owner, AAA Coaches of Kirknewton, and is seen here at Glasgow University on a wet day in July 2014. It carries the first Shuttle Coaches livery and is pictured on the cover of this book in the later style. (BN)

PO11HVW was a later purchase from EVE Coaches of Dunbar. These two were built as high-capacity coaches from new and look so much better internally than upseated conversions. Both are at the Odeon in Kilmarnock on 16/06/17 along with a Javelin and a Solo. (LM)

Another SR Solo bought new is YD63VDY, seen waiting for passengers at Croftfoot Road, Glasgow, on 29/05/20. It is working service M2 to Toryglen, a route temporarily taken over from First Glasgow during the COVID-19 epidemic. (MC)

The Largs local service was bought from an Ardrossan operator that couldn't finance the conversion to low-floor operation. Short SE Solo MX08DHE came from Dawsonrentals, originally keeping its white paintwork with extensive route branding. It is seen in less than pristine condition on a wintry day in March 2018 with the Cumbrae ferry in the background. (LM)

Volvo B9R YN09DXH was bought because its Plaxton Panther body incorporated a wheelchair lift and the market for accessible coaches is growing. It is gingerly boarding the *Isle of Cumbrae* at Portavadie on 12/10/19.

The final SPT-supplied MyBus vehicle type was the 7.8m Solo, typified by YJ15AOA on its regular working, the M13 in Ayr on 27/07/18. (BN)

Another Panther was TK07ADK, a Volvo B12 from the defunct Kinch of Minety fleet. It ran in Kinch's blue and cream livery for a few months before being re-liveried and re-registered GSU483. (LM)

YJ66AOK was part of a cancelled order from an Australian customer allowing Optare to deliver at short notice – not normally their strong point – and we needed another Solo urgently. It is unique among the twenty-one Solos in the fleet in having a Cummins 6-cylinder engine; the other twenty have Mercedes' almost indestructible OM904. (DG)

Solo YJ16DYB heads along the coast at Ardrossan working service M22 when nearly new. One more Solo, YJ66AOF, arrived before SPT abandoned their policy of supplying vehicles. This was rather ironic as they had eventually got it right after providing unsuitable buses for five very difficult years. (RK)

Coming from Megabus, SF59FYX was the first tri-axle in the fleet since the Talbots left in 1993 but is of a slightly larger scale, accommodating 73 passengers in its 15 metres. Used mainly on a school contract, it does see use on private hires despite its thirst for diesel, as here at Glasgow Science Centre on 16/11/17. (LM)

At the opposite end of the scale in the Shuttle Coaches fleet is L15SBL, a Mercedes 311 Sprinter. Although it was bought for a school contract, it is frequently out in the evenings and weekends on private hire work, as here in 2019. (RG)

We sampled, and discarded, the Cheetah XL which was Plaxton's rather unsatisfactory attempt at building a minicoach on the Mercedes 921L Atego chassis. Consequently, we returned to Turas who supplied YN67CCZ. It wasn't too long ago when £135,000 would have bought a new 53-seater, but this is what it gets you now! It was still cold in Largs on 02/03/18 as it waited at the ferry terminal. (LM)

We bought a second KingLong, BX63ZSX, which is a shorter XMQ6120C, as a repossession at a knockdown price in 2018. Most of our school contracts are with East Ayrshire Council, who have age restrictions on school buses, so the opportunity to buy a five-year-old school bus for less than the price of the equivalent 10-year-old Volvo was too good to miss.

A significant addition to the service bus fleet in 2018 was LM18URG, a Mellor Strata Mercedes Sprinter, for new subsidised service 347 between Rankinston and Ayr. This is a demanding route operating for seventeen hours a day seven days a week and the Strata has proved up to the job. It is less than two months old in this view at Burns Statue Square, Ayr, on 03/09/18. (BN)

Solo YD63UZK arrived from CHC Helicopters at Aberdeen heliport. It had spent four years as a spare airside-only vehicle, hence the orange light on the roof, and had less than 10,000 miles on the clock. (RG)

DVLA insisted the original registration was invalid and reissued it with SE62XFN, inexplicable for a vehicle built in 2014, but after arguing with them for eight months we gave in. It was operating service 74 in Carmunnock Road, Glasgow, on 29/05/20, covering a First Glasgow route during the COVID-19 emergency. (MC)

Additional school contract work was won in 2019 following the closure of Milton Coaches, Kilbirnie, and led to the acquisition of Transit HN16XOY, seen here on a hire at Ardgowan House, Inverkip. (RG)

Two Solos previously owned by Flintshire Council were bought unseen at auction in 2019. YJ56ATK was repainted in orange as a backup for the MyBus fleet, although it is more often found working the Stewarton local service as here on 25/05/20. We had briefly operated this vehicle way back in 2006 when it was an Optare demonstrator. (RK)

In 2019 two Scanias were bought from a finance company auction following the liquidation of Harlequin Coaches of Broxburn. As its registration suggests, Scania/Irizar PB FA62ENG was previously used by the English Football Association. The paintwork was too good to repaint so it gained a more subtle version of the Shuttle Coaches graphics, as seen here in Stratford Upon Avon. (DA)

A second Mellor Strata arrived in April 2019 as LL19PWO. It was followed by six more in July, LO19WBL, WBM, WBN, WBP, WBT & WBU, after a large MyBus contract in Glasgow was picked up at very short notice. The COVID-19 pandemic in 2020 led to the suspension of all MyBus services, with the Stratas being redeployed onto local service work. LO19WBT is seen in Newlands, Glasgow, on 27/05/20 operating service 29 between Newton Mearns and Shawlands, which had been abandoned by First Glasgow. (MC)

Two for the price of one - McGill's Strata LO67CGV is seen at Avenue Square, Stewarton, heading for Kilmarnock on service 337. Sitting behind it is our LO19WBL which had been reallocated to the Stewarton local service, having lost its normal MyBus duties. (RK)

With Main Street in Largs almost deserted, LO19WBM has found its way onto service 40, the Largs local, one of the few routes which the company operates on a wholly commercial basis. Because of the large numbers of retired people living in the town who enjoy free travel, it is not unusual for this service to bring in less than £10 a day from fare-paying passengers. (RK)

The graveyard behind the garage is the resting place of stored vehicles and others being broken for spares. Optare Solo YK05CAA came from Flintshire Council via auction, and VW Tucana YX09HRE was an off-lease MyBus vehicle bought from SPT. Neither was ever operated, although our first two Tucanas were close relations – YX09HRF and HRG. (DG)

Another former SPT vehicle is Solo YJ57YCF. This bus was converted into a mobile travel centre and became an aborted project to fit a hybrid drive. We bought the remains mainly for the engine, which will be transplanted into one of our fleet in due course. Orion YX13BWC is just visible on the right, its working life over after engine failure. (DG)

Hire-ins and Demonstrators

Unsurprisingly we were not on many people's radar in the early years of the business and it wasn't until 2005 that we were offered our first demonstrator, a Solo that we unsuspectingly bought at auction fourteen years later!

In the early days, a source of short-term leased coaches was Bus and Coach Rentals, whose vehicles we used on occasion when our own let us down, one such being ex-Western Seddon Pennine DSD982V. Western themselves lent us Leyland Leopard TSJ79S to cover a short-term school contract. Much later, as Dial-A-Bus work developed, we hired in buses from Mistral to cover contracts awarded to us at very short notice – a mix of Mercedes Plaxton Beavers and Optare Solos. Once we began buying Solos, Optare were more forthcoming and a variety of Solo demonstrators passed through the fleet, often while we were awaiting new vehicles on order. An Excel was provided for the same reason, although we were distinctly unimpressed by its fuel consumption. Plaxton did try to tempt us away from Optare in 2006, lending us a Primo, but like most operators we were not swayed.

More recently, the big manufacturers have seemed to take a bit more notice of us and SR Solos, two ADL Enviro 200s (one the stylish MMC version), a Wrightbus Streetlight and two similar Nu-Trak Vibes have all been provided as demonstrators and used extensively on local service and MyBus work. In 2012 we operated a contract for the Senior Open Golf championship at Turnberry using two demonstrators, a Solo and an Enviro 200, and just one of our own vehicles! An all-electric Solo EV was trialled for a month in 2019 but it could only manage half a shift on a charge. We were not sufficiently impressed by any of the competition to move away from the Solo until the arrival of the Strata.

M14
DIAL A BUS
SHUTTLE BUSES
OPTARE
MW52 PYP

W997 JNF

500
SHUTTLE BUSES
OPTARE

OPTARE

113
SHUTTLE BUSES
OPTARE

Not In Service
Primo
YN06 CYE

OPTARE
YJ56 ATK

NU-TRACK LTD DEMONSTRATOR T: 028 944 69550
38

NU-TRACK LTD DEMONSTRATOR T: 028 944 69550
Nu-Vibe
LRZ 3094

EV

Irvine Cross 29
YX17 NXA

Acknowledgments

My thanks to everybody who has contributed to this book. Lawrence Macduff and George Heaney have provided invaluable assistance, particularly with research into the early history of the business where my memory is somewhat cloudy. Des Bradshaw, who has overseen the maintenance of the majority of these buses, has helped me with the technical details and Rachel Granger has enhanced many of the pictures – most of these photos date from well before the era of digital photography.

A number of photographers have freely contributed images and my thanks go to them all. I have been pleasantly surprised by the large number of pictures which have been made available to me, and the early days are very well represented. The company's archive of pictures is now into four figures and there are very few vehicles which we have owned where I don't have a photo – doubtless the gaps will be filled in due course.

Where known, photographers are:

WMG	Bill McGregor	AD	Alistair Douglas	RG	Ross Granger
LM	Lawrence Macduff	RK	Robert Kelly	DA	Danny Armstrong
MC	Murdoch Currie	DD	David Devoy	DG	author
SB	Stewart Brown	BN	Billy Nichol		

HAMILTON
6832 RDS

Stewarton 113
via Kilmaurs
SHUTTLE BUSES
YJ66 AOK